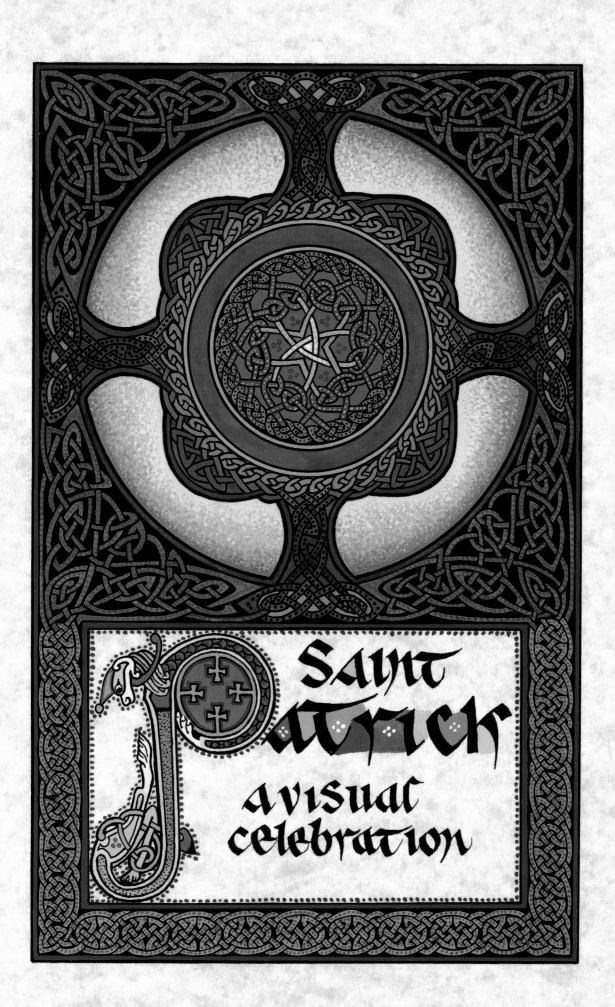

Saint Patrick
a visual celebration

libris

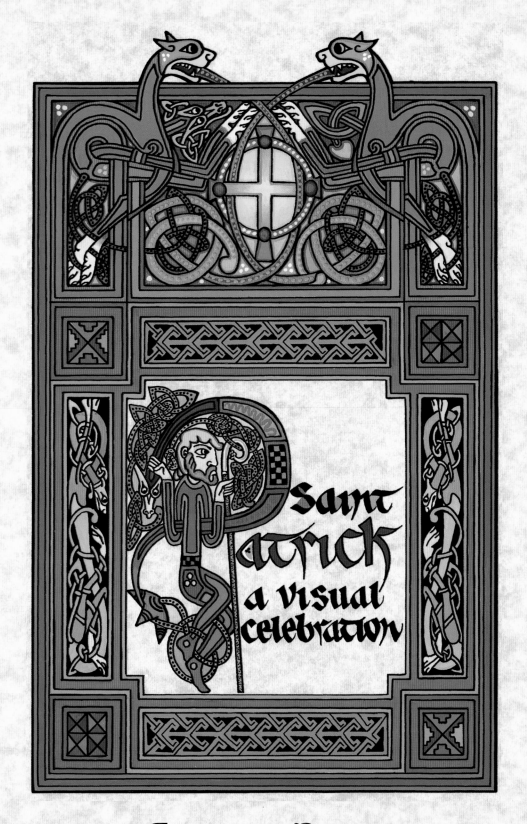

Saint Patrick
a visual celebration

Courtney Davis
Text by Elaine Gill and Dennis O'Neill

BLANDFORD

Dedication

This book is dedicated to the Celtic Spirit
and the many unseen inspirers who guide
my pen and brush.

And to the memory of Bob Elford.

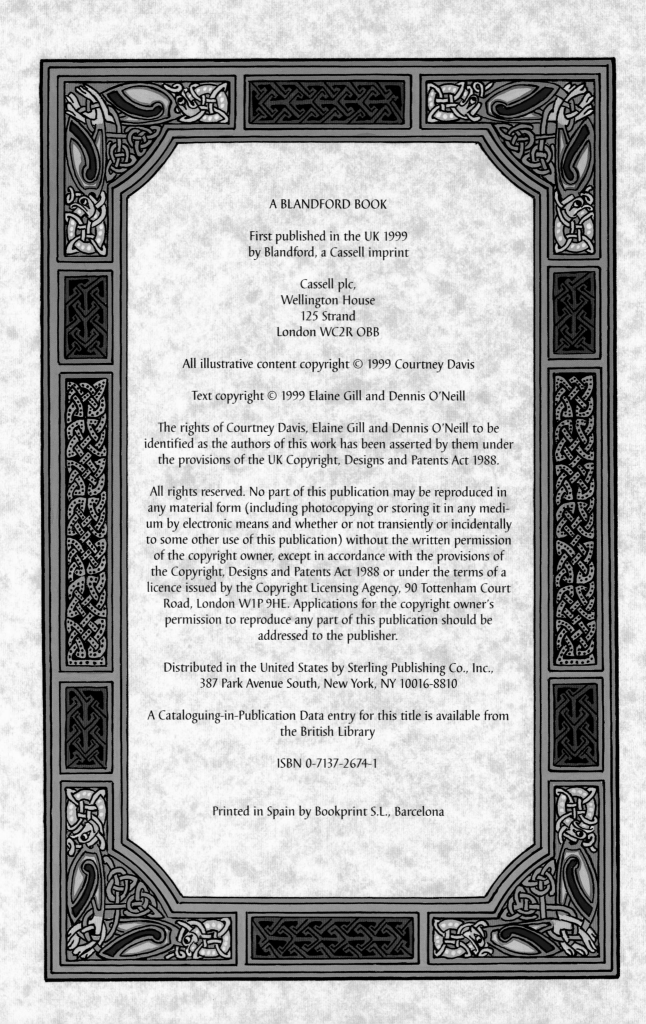

A BLANDFORD BOOK

First published in the UK 1999
by Blandford, a Cassell imprint

Cassell plc,
Wellington House
125 Strand
London WC2R OBB

Distributed in the United States by Sterling Publishing Co., Inc.,
387 Park Avenue South, New York, NY 10016-8810

A Cataloguing-in-Publication Data entry for this title is available from
the British Library

ISBN 0-7137-2674-1

Printed in Spain by Bookprint S.L., Barcelona

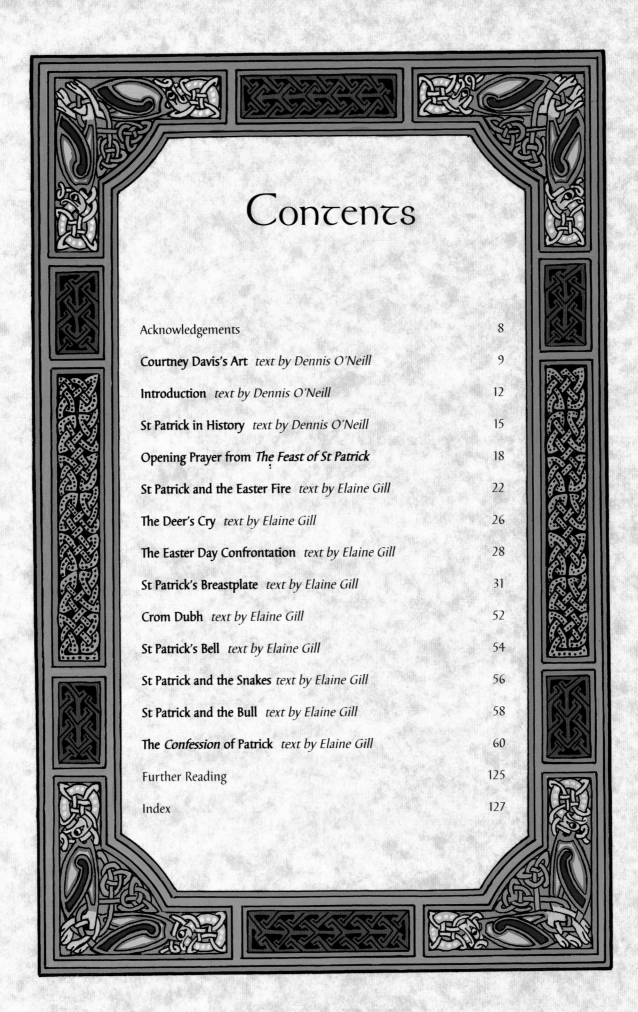

Contents

Acknowledgements

My grateful thanks to Father Dennis O'Neill and Elaine Gill for the text in this book and also to Thomas Kinsella for the use of the 'Breastplate'.

The 'Opening Prayer' from *The Feast of St Patrick* on page 18 is reproduced by kind permission of A.P. Watt Ltd on behalf of The Hierarchies of England and Wales, Ireland and Australia.

I should also like to thank those people in Chicago who I met in September 1997 and whose enthusiasm for the paintings in this book inspired me and gave me the energy to complete it on my return. Thanks also to my agents Mike and Laura Elliott and Marc Duro, who has already begun to transfer my work into stained glass in his own unique way, and to Dave Merron.

Finally, thanks to my long-suffering family and loyal friends who put up with me disappearing into the studio for long periods of time to complete these projects.

Courtney Davis's Art

In the autumn of 1997, I was privileged to witness what happens when the veil separating this world from the Otherworld is lifted and living humans have a glimpse of Paradise. Amazingly, this happened in my own dining room! Courtney Davis was visiting the United States for a fortnight and spent a weekend in my rectory. I am aware that, in the Celtic understanding of reality, the body is in the soul of the person. Without even intending to do so, before a gathering of around 30 people, Courtney actually managed to help those present to 'see' this. With the use of dowsing rods, he measured the precise parameters of the energy fields around different individuals. He showed us how our energy fields contract as we either close in on ourselves, or shut down altogether and expand proportionately as we feel joyous and expansive. He gave any potential sceptics an opportunity to test this out for themselves if they wished. He then took one of his own pictures and invited individuals to concentrate on it, allowing themselves to be drawn into its world. In each case, their energy fields expanded dramatically.

Witnessing this heightened my appreciation of the way many branches of Eastern Christianity use the veneration of icons as a means of drawing the believer into closer communion either with Christ or whichever angel or saint is depicted. A similar principle is operating in both cases: Celtic images, designs and mandalas and Eastern Christian icons are all gateways through which a believer can enter the Otherworld and deeper communion with its inhabitants.

Before the evening ended, Courtney also measured the energy field around the picture itself and then, speaking the entire time, slowly approached the picture to show what happens when he crosses the boundary of a picture's energy field and enters its world. As he crossed over his voice began to change, distorting into a deeper sound and slowing down. It became increasingly muffled as he approached the picture.

As he backed away from the picture, his voice returned to normal. It seemed to me that I was being given a glimpse of what happens when someone enters 'the mists of Avalon' and passes through the 'veil' which separates this world from the Otherworld. The Celtic Otherworld is the real studio which Courtney enters whenever he prepares to paint one of his marvellous pictures. Its inhabitants are his teachers and guides as he puts brush to the page. The next morning, after celebrating the Eucharistic liturgy, several parishioners came to the rectory for coffee and sweets. Courtney invited them into the dining room, where he opened the velvet satchel in which he kept the artwork for *Saint Patrick – A Visual Celebration.* He began to display the pages across the surface of the table, one next to the other, until the whole surface was covered. The exposure of each page was accompanied by audible exclamations of wonder from some and deepening silence from others. In the end there was complete silence. People just kept gazing, soaking up the beauty, as if they could not take it all in.

In the Celtic belief system, there are times in the year when the veil separating this world from the other is considered to be thinner than at other times. It is believed that, at these times, it is easier for humans to slip from one side to the other. The quarterly lunar festivals are such times. It is thought that the thinnest space of all comes at Samhain, the Celtic New Year, which takes place on the night between Hallowe'en and All Saints' Day.

Perhaps Courtney Davis can pass through the 'veil' so effortlessly because he is himself a Celt, born to parents of Welsh, Scottish and Irish descent on 31 October 1946. While his birthplace was Blackwood, South Wales, he grew up in London. Alas, throughout his life he has suffered from back problems and is registered as disabled. After three years of employment as a designer for one of England's largest jewellery manufacturers, he was in such pain that he had to have major spinal surgery in order to keep going. It was during the painful period immediately after his initial surgery that he had the first of a series of mystical experiences which completely changed his life. It began with the sensation that his departed grandmother was manipulating and massaging his left leg and foot, which had lost feeling from the surgery, in order to accelerate the healing process. This was followed by a vision in which the wall suddenly opened up, allowing the hospital ward to be filled with radiant light, smoke and Otherworld beings. These were monks, who surrounded him and began a three-hour operation, manipulating and cutting out sections of his back, and replacing them a few minutes later. Whenever they were working on any of its inner parts they lifted him above his own body. This extraordinary experience had a threefold result. Even though he eventually had to have more back surgery, he has been well enough to have maintained a continuous creative output for the last 20 years. In 1987, after creating black and white images for the previous ten years, he began to paint wonderful things with the aid of spirit lights which guided his hand.

Entirely self-taught, using gouache and ink, he has turned out more and more remarkable Celtic art, in a flow that has been ever-cascading and ever-fresh in imagination and design. Over 20 books have resulted thus far, culminating in his present masterpiece, *Saint Patrick – A Visual Celebration*. Just as the ancient Druids and bards went through 20 years of rigorous training before they were considered fully qualified to practise their skills, so Courtney feels that, in producing this book, his art is now being elevated to a new level of maturity. He has also found that he has an ability which can be used in healing, and worked successfully in various churches and hospitals until his art took up more and more of his time. Courtney's life's work is being launched into a new future, where his artistic outpouring will be guided even more manifestly by, and give access more easily to, the Celtic Otherworld from which it emerges.

Dennis O'Neill

Introduction

The longer I live, the more I appreciate St Patrick. He is much more multifaceted to me, a priest, than the saint to whom I was introduced as a child growing up in Chicago. At this point in my life, he has become an important symbol of hope.

I was raised in a family who traced most of its ancestry to Ireland. With a surname like O'Neill, we felt little need to demonstrate our Irishness; and we took it for granted that Patrick was one of history's greatest saints. We were quite smug about these things. We were also smug, but wrongly so, in assuming that 'Irish Christian' and 'Roman Catholic' had always been synonymous terms. In other words, behind my religious training there was much that was either suppressed, forgotten, or simply never mentioned.

I was an adolescent in the 1960s and was involved in the anti-establishment protests, which in those days were so much a part of American campus life. I was also in seminary at the time, so my protests were not only against my nation's involvement in the Vietnam War, but also against what I considered to be some of the narrower and more judgemental aspects of my Church, which identifies itself as Catholic – 'Universal'. The Second Vatican Council evolved during that decade, and, in the wake of the liturgical and other changes which resulted, I was left with the heady, narcissistic sense that the Church would eventually change everything with which I was in disagreement. In those days, several branches of Christianity began to reappraise themselves, and many became less inclined to demonize expressions of Christianity which had thus far not been embraced by their own particular denominations. Some branches of the Christian family actually began to listen and to learn from each other. Since the Roman Church no longer required the identical Latin Eucharistic celebration everywhere, its liturgies began to take on local flavours. The pace of all this change was too much for some and not rapid enough for others. Thus, many people began either to entrench themselves in conservative reaction, shift denominations, discontinue active participation in the Church, or even to revert to pre-Christian expressions of faith.

This could all have been bewildering – indeed, overwhelming – to one who treasures his Catholic identity but desires that his Church become as all-embracing as its name implies. By then, however, I knew more about both St Patrick and about the Celtic Church, which developed as a result of his vision.

By the generation after his death, primarily because of Patrick, most of Ireland had embraced a Christianity that was both completely orthodox and simultaneously unlike Christianity anywhere else on earth. This was due to his ability to hold on to what is essential about Christianity while drawing people to that faith by offering a wider, more unconditionally welcoming embrace than any other missionary until modern times.

Being a Celt himself, he understood Celtic people. Before Patrick was ever carried off into Irish slavery, he was already as familiar with the great festivals of the Celtic pre-Christian calendar as he was with the Christian feasts which his own family would have observed. Being a romanized Briton, he grew up in a family which had been Christian for at least the previous two generations. Their Christianity had most likely come by way of Gaul, where the theology was Roman and the monastic asceticism had its origins in either Egypt, Palestine or Syria. His own theological training was also Roman, but this did not prevent him from being open to religious syncretism. In this, he was a pioneer.

Patrick was unique among Christian missionaries not only because of the love he developed for his former captors, but also because he blended it with the deep respect he already had for the pre-Christian culture, its legal system and its religion. He admired the learning and the spiritual methods of the bards and the Druids. His own abilities as a shapeshifter and – at Druidic showdowns – a wonder-worker strongly hint that he acquired some Druidic skills himself. He did not attack the pre-Christian Celtic faith. Rather, he presumed that, if Christianity was in any way superior to it, these seekers of wisdom and truth would welcome Christ as the fulfilment of their desires. Patrick's mission embraced as much of Celtic spiritual custom and practice as would complement Christianity; he 'baptized' the holy wells, the festivals, and whatever else

13

he could. With the Celtic beliefs that divinity is often experienced in triune form – like the triple-goddess Brigid – that there is surely a blessed Afterlife, and that those who have preceded us there are still very close to us, the Irish had no problem with the Christian doctrines of the Holy Trinity, Heaven and the Communion of Saints.

To my contemporaries who have left Catholicism because they consider that its Romanness has compromised its Catholicity, or have left Christianity because they consider it to be too patriarchal and anti-ecological, I would offer St Patrick and the Celtic Church as it existed in Ireland shortly after his death as a sign of hope. They are a reminder that there was for centuries a Western branch of Christianity in which everyone so loved nature that they generally worshipped outdoors; in which women and men treated each other with more equality than any-where else in continental Europe at the time; in which Patrick's disciple, St Mel, the first abbotbishop of Ardagh, ordained St Brigid of Kildare, a bishop; in which there were married as well as celibate clergy; in which the rotation of the seasons was celebrated.

The business of spirituality is finding and making connections. If words like 'ecumenical', 'inter-faith' and 'global village' have become symbols of hope for the unity of human beings and of our shifting from mutual antagonism to mutual understanding, then Patrick and the Celtic Church could serve as a channel through which Christianity and the New Age movement, the ecological movement, and even shamanism, astrology and neo-pagan earth-centred religion – subjects presently forbidden to most Christians – could begin to enter into a genuine healing dialogue.

Even though a great deal has already been written about Patrick, Courtney Davis's contribution here is unique. He offers excerpts from the saint's own writings in a way that honours Patrick's special achieve-ment. Presented in the style of Irish illuminated manuscripts, the texts take on a new life. This is exactly what happened when the bardic tradition of verbal embellishment was put into writing – a syncretism which had its origin in Patrick's evangelical vision. I think Patrick would be very pleased.

Dennis O'Neill

St Patrick in History

In the history of Christian missions, St Patrick holds an honoured, unique place: no one else's evangelistic style succeeded so remarkably. His first experience of Ireland revealed a people who, for the most part, were either unaware of Christianity or thought of it as an alien faith. By the generation after his death, primarily because of him, most of the nation had embraced a Christianity which was both completely orthodox and, simultaneously, unlike Christianity anywhere else on earth. This was due both to his compassion and to his ability to hold on to what is essential about Christianity, while drawing people to that faith by offering a wider, more unconditionally welcoming embrace than any other missionary until modern times.

A Celt himself, Patrick understood the Celtic people. Being a romanized Briton, his actual name was Magonus Succatus Patricius. His father had been both a deacon and decurion and his grandfather a priest. Their Christianity probably came from Gaul, where the theology was Roman and the monastic asceticism brought there by St John Cassian was either Syrian, Palestinian or Egyptian. The Romans had not yet entirely pulled out of Britain, so Patrick grew up in a world whose mores and Christianity were provincial Roman - albeit on the extreme northwest frontier of the Empire, in an area which had never lost its Celtic identity and customs. Before Patrick was carried off into Irish slavery, he had already become familiar with the Celtic festivals of the pre-Christian calendar which his own family would have observed. While the men in his family were ordained, they do not appear to have been fanatical about their faith. Even Patrick describes himself as being rather indifferent to it as a youth.

His abduction at the age of 16 by an Irish raiding party changed everything. During six years of enslavement he developed a life of prayer, and attributed his eventual escape to the help of God. Most of his story is well known. He returned to Ireland as a missionary, whose training and Christian background were primarily Roman. Christian missionaries such as St Palladius had come to Ireland earlier than Patrick, bringing a Christianity similarly Roman in style, but apparently with little

success. So why did Patrick succeed where others had failed? Perhaps the critical difference was that he learned to love the Irish people genuinely. By blending that love with the deep respect he already had for Celtic pre-Christian culture, its legal system and its religion, he won them over. While he wrote that his apostolate was no 'unbroken series of peaceful triumphs' and that he and his companions were imprisoned and several times in peril of their lives, there is nevertheless no nation whose conversion to Christianity produced martyrs as few in number as Ireland.

Perhaps because his own kidnapping had prevented him from completing his education and had left him self-conscious about being unlettered, Patrick admired the learning and the spiritual methods of the bards and the Druids. If there is even a core of truth in the fabulous legends which developed around him, it seems he may have learned many of their methods himself. Later writers described him as a shapeshifter and – at Druidic showdowns – a wonder-worker nearly comparable to Moses before Pharaoh.

According to the *Annals of Ulster*, Patrick's mission to Ireland began in the year 432. His earliest *Lives* were written in the late seventh century. Since all his biographical material is very much later, it is especially fortunate that two documents remain, and which were written by Patrick himself. Both his *Confession* and his *Letter to Coroticus* reveal him to have been an honest, humble, courageous and sensitive man of deep faith.

Since the sort of Christianity Patrick brought to Ireland was Romano-British, it is remarkable that as early as the beginning of the sixth century the customs of Irish Christianity were so distinctly and uniquely Celtic. Thus they remained until they were officially suppressed by the Synod of Whitby in 664. Even after this Synod, in some parts of the Celtic world, Roman observances were not accepted for centuries. The Celts celebrated Easter on a date other than the rest of the Christian West. They had no Roman diocesan system, but rather large communities of monks and nuns on the Celtic tribal model, with the abbots and abbesses as the supreme jurisdictional authorities and the bishops being generally relegated only to their sacramental function. The monks' tonsure was Druidic: the front of the head was shaved, rather than the crown. Since they loved nature, worship generally took place outdoors rather than in churches. Indeed, with hardly any exceptions, there were no large churches at all – only small chapels.

Some of these differences can be attributed to the way in which the independent Celtic spirit was attracted to and adopted the autonomous monastic customs of the Syrian and Egyptian desert communities, which had been introduced by way of Gaul. But the Irish themselves credit the rest to St Patrick.

What eventually became the Celtic cross was originally a symbol of the divine sun-wheel, combined with the world's axis and primordial mountain. This kind of conversion came more from a change of religious perception than from a belligerent clashing of two faiths. No wonder Patrick was so successful!

Opening Prayer from
The Feast of St Patrick

God our Father,
you sent St Patrick
to preach your glory to
the people of Ireland.

By the help of his prayers
may all Christians
proclaim your love
to all men.

Grant this through
our Lord Jesus Christ,
your Son,
who lives and reigns
with you and the
Holy Spirit,
one God,
for ever and ever.

Your Father,
you sent St. Patrick
to preach your glory to
the people of Ireland.

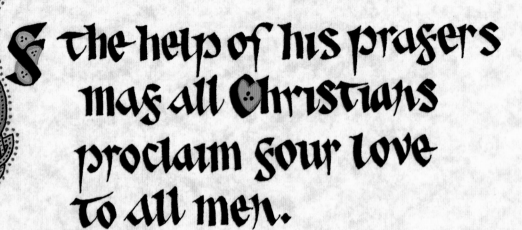

S the help of his prayers
may all Christians
proclaim your love
to all men.

rant this through
our lord Jesus Christ,
your Son,
who lives and reigns
with you and the
holy Spirit,
one God,
for ever and ever.

21

St Patrick and the Easter Fire

The land lay in complete darkness. Not a fire burned, nor was there a flame to be seen anywhere. It was an important time of the year in ancient Ireland – a sacred spring feast when the royal fire would be lit and would blaze out over the countryside in celebration, proclaiming the power of the royal line. All lights and fires had been extinguished in preparation for the special moment when the royal flame would leap into life and the ceremony begin. It was forbidden for anyone in any part of the kingdom to light a fire before the one kindled in the king's own house, and a proclamation to this effect had been issued throughout the country. Consequently, no one dared to defy this law, on pain of death.

And so it was that the high king Leoghaire, son of Niall, and his court, accompanied by a great gathering of other kings and governors and noble visitors, sat in darkness at Tara, the royal seat, awaiting this momentous event. There was an expectant silence; no one stirred. Suddenly it grew lighter, and turning towards the brightness, the people, to their amazement and fear, saw a point of light burning on the distant Hill of Slane across the plains of Meath, about 12 miles away. What outrage was this? Who would dare to do such a thing? What did it mean?

An apprehensive shiver went through the crowd. The wise men and counsellors were quickly summoned to advise on the happening, but in their bewilderment they protested that they did not know who had done the deed and violated the tradition. But the wizards of the court declared, 'O great king, live for ever. This fire which has been lit on the Hill of Slane before your fire here on the Hill of Tara will never be put out unless it is extinguished this very night. Even more, it will be greater than the power of our fire, and the one who lit it

will overcome us all, even you, and will win over all the men of your land, and all the kingdoms will be subject to it, for it will fill all things and reign for ever!' This is how the divine fire lit by St Patrick to celebrate the Christian festival of Easter was described.

King Leoghaire was well aware of the new faith that was spreading through his land, and how the old traditions and knowledge were being threatened by it. Indeed, his own son, Fedilmid, and his grandson, Fortchern, had become Christians. The words of the wizards deeply disturbed the king, and the people of the court too, for their power was being challenged. In consternation Leoghaire cried out, 'No, it shall not be! We will go now and put an end to the matter. We shall arrest and put to death those who are responsible for this sacrilege against our kingdom.' He called his two most senior wizards, Lucetmael and Lochru, and bade them accompany him to confront the perpetrator of this outrage. As the tradition of their gods demanded, 27 chariots were yoked for the journey to Slane.

On the way, the wizards warned the king that he must not go too near the fire but should keep his distance, thus showing his superiority over Patrick, and also so that he would not be mistaken for a Christian worshipper. They said, 'O great King, let him be summoned to attend you, so that he will pay his respects to you and you will be lord and master. We will talk with him where you can see us, and thus prove ourselves to you.' The king considered, and agreeing with their plan did not immediately go to the site of the fire when they reached Slane, but dismounted and sat down nearby.

St Patrick was bidden to come to King Leoghaire outside the enclosure, and to show their supremacy over the saint the wizards determined not to stand up at his approach. After some time, Patrick came towards them singing loudly from Psalm 19, 'Some may go in chariots and some on horses, but we will walk in the name of our God.' As planned they remained seated, except for one man called Erc, son of Daeg, who was sure that St Patrick had the true faith. He was moved to rise and salute the holy man who stretched out his hand and blessed him, and from that moment Erc became a Christian.

Then Patrick began to converse with the wizards. Lochru was particularly insolent and haughty. He scoffed at Patrick's teachings, abusing and belittling the new faith. This made Patrick angry, and he reacted by calling on God to send retribution and destroy the opposing wizard for his blasphemy. An unseen force tore Lochru up into the air and then dropped him from a great height so that he fell head-first, smashing his skull against a stone. His death alarmed the people, and filled them with dread and horror.

The Deer's Cry

Not only were King Leoghaire and his followers shocked and frightened, but they were very angry and even more determined to kill St Patrick. Realizing the threat, and that they were about to attack him, he declared, 'May God arise and His enemies be scattered, and those who hate Him flee from His face.' At once a darkness fell. A thick, menacing blackness descended upon them, and instead of setting on Patrick and his band, Leoghaire's men turned on each other, man against man, injuring and killing. Chaos ensued. A mighty earthquake shook the ground, causing the waiting chariots and horses to career violently across the flat plain at break neck speed. A few survivors, barely alive, escaped the death and destruction and took refuge in the mountains.

The aftermath of Patrick's curse was that only the king and seven other people were left on the Hill of Slane, namely his wife, two other kings and four subjects. All were terrified after this display of devastation. The queen begged Patrick not to destroy her husband, King Leoghaire, promising that he would come and kneel down and worship the Christian God. The king was driven by fear to comply, but only pretended to pay homage. He still desperately wanted to destroy the saint, especially after the humiliation he had just suffered at his hands. King Leoghaire separated himself from the little group of remaining people and called Patrick over to him, with the intention of doing him harm. However, the saint was aware of the monarch's evil designs and knew it was a trick.

Turning towards his own companions, consisting of eight men and a young boy, he raised his hand and blessed them in the name of Jesus Christ. Then an amazing thing happened. As King Leoghaire counted them, nine in number, they immediately became invisible to him! Instead he saw a group of eight deer and a young fawn trotting away into the countryside.

At length, dejected, saddened and defeated, Leoghaire and his small retinue returned to Tara at dawn.

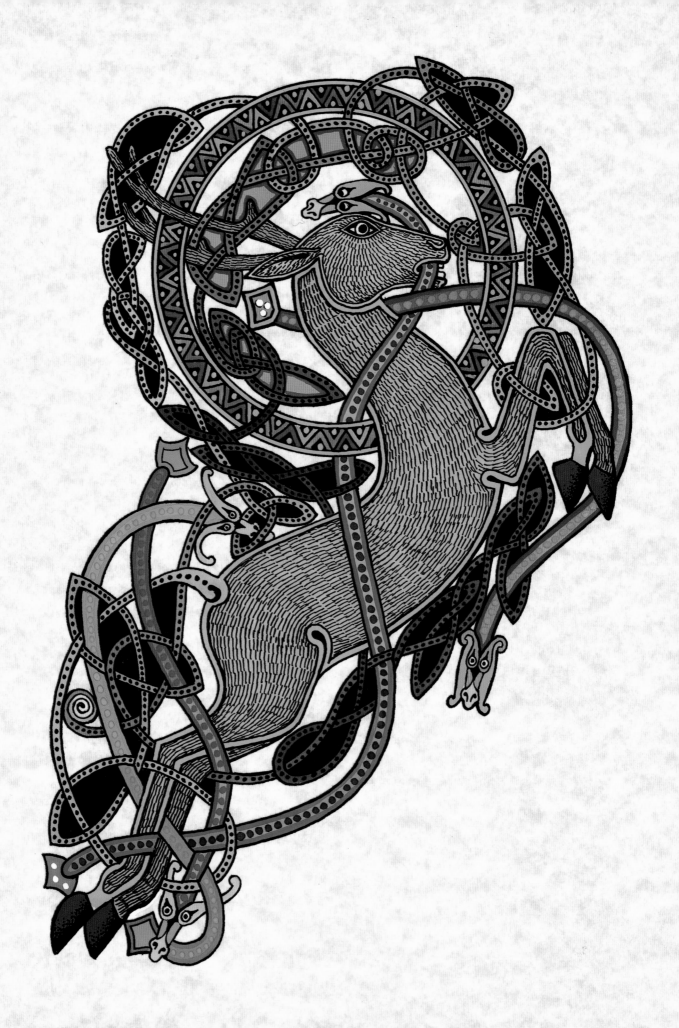

The Easter Day Confrontation

The pagan spring festival continued into the next day and King Leoghaire and his court were taking their leisure, feasting and drinking wine in the royal household at Tara, and talking over the catastrophic events of the previous night. For Patrick and his fellow Christians it was Easter Day, the most important celebration of the year, and the saint and five companions travelled to Tara to challenge Leoghaire and preach the Gospel to him and his people.

They found all the doors barred against them, but were able to gain entrance to the royal banqueting hall, miraculously passing right through the closed gates. Only one man in the assembly rose to honour St Patrick, a poet named Dubthach maccu Lugil, who in later life became a Christian bishop. Surprisingly and hospitably, the king invited Patrick and his followers to enjoy the feast and to eat freely.

The wizard Lucetmael saw the opportunity to seek revenge for the untimely death of his companion Lochru, and challenged St Patrick to a further contest of powers. Before all those present he poured something from his own drinking vessel into that of the saint. Patrick blessed his cup and the liquid in it froze and became solid, so that when he turned it upside-down only the drop of poison added by the sorcerer splashed on to the ground. He blessed the cup a second time and the contents became liquid once more, at which all the people marvelled.

Thwarted, Lucetmael suggested that they should each bring snow to the surrounding plain, to test the strength of their respective magical abilities. St Patrick stated that he would not do something that was against the will of God, but Lucetmael, with incantations, conjured up waist-deep snow, to everyone's amazement. 'We have all seen your power,' said the saint, 'now take the snow away.' But the wizard replied that he could not make the snow vanish until the following day. 'You are able to do wicked things but not good ones, unlike me,' said Patrick, and as he blessed the land the snow disappeared immediately without trace.

Next, the king's magician summoned evil spirits and commanded a heavy darkness to cover the land. 'Drive away this blackness,' demanded St Patrick, and when Lucetmael could not do so, the saint dispersed it with a prayer, enabling the sun to shine once more.

King Leoghaire had watched the progress of the contest very closely and desired a decisive trial as conclusive proof of the superior power of one of the rivals. He commanded, 'Each of you must throw your books into the water, and the one whose property emerges undamaged will be the victor.' Patrick agreed immediately, but the wizard protested that he would not take part in a trial by water, as the saint regarded water as his God. Here Lucetmael was referring to the practice of Christian baptism. The king then suggested that instead of water, fire should be used. Again Patrick confidently concurred, but once again the wizard refused, mistakenly saying that the saint also worshipped fire.

Now it was Patrick's turn to put forward an idea. His suggestion was readily accepted and a wooden hut was quickly built in two sections, one half made of green, freshly cut wood, and the other of older, dry timber. Lucetmael, wearing Patrick's cloak, entered the green side of the little house and one of Patrick's disciples, a boy called Benignus, entered the dry side, wearing the wizard's outer garment. Then, before the assembled crowd, the building was set alight. Although the odds seemed heavily weighted in favour of Lucetmael, he was utterly consumed in the blaze and only Patrick's mantle remained unscathed, whereas Benignus and the dry half of the hut were left intact, except for the sorcerer's robe which was burned.

This further death enraged King Leoghaire, and he determined once more to destroy St Patrick. However, the saint knew of the king's plans and averted the danger by prayer, warning him that he would soon die if he did not change his ways and believe in the true God. The king and all his people were terrified by Patrick's prediction, and Leoghaire, consulting his wise men and advisers, agreed that it would be better to believe than to die, and so they finally accepted the Christian faith. However, St Patrick prophesied that because the king had so stubbornly opposed his teachings and had been such an obstacle to him, even though he would continue to reign, no one of his line would become king after him.

St Patrick's Breastplate

The ancient incantation known as 'St Patrick's Breastplate' has several other titles including the Irish name 'Faeth Fiada'. This has been mistranslated as 'The Deer's Cry' and is linked with the story, told in Muirchu's *Life of the Saint*, of how Patrick and his followers changed themselves into the likeness of deer to escape danger. However, the name probably relates to a specific spell or charm used to facilitate shapeshifting into the form of deer.

This prayer is part of a long tradition of prayers of protection stemming from pre-Christian times. These are called *loricae*, the plural of the Latin word *lorica* for a leather cuirass or a protective body covering. Despite some of the invocations having distinctly pagan echoes, St Patrick's Breastplate is deeply Christian in its expression. In St Paul's 'Letter to the Ephesians' there is a precedent for this type of prayer, where the disciple is urged to 'put on the whole armour of God', including the 'breastplate of righteousness'.

Linguistically this lorica cannot be traced back further than the eighth century, and this raises the question of whether it was based on an earlier poem dating back to the time of St Patrick in the fifth century, or whether it was actually completely unknown to the saint, although it has been ascribed to him. In one sense it does not matter if Patrick was the author, because the prayer so eloquently portrays the spirit and vigour of early Christianity in Ireland, where Christ is not shown as the Saviour who comes to rescue a sinful and fallen world, but as one who releases a wonderful and sanctified creation from subjection, and scatters the darkness with His light. It is not about duality and death, but unity and wholeness.

St Patrick's Breastplate

Translation by Thomas Kinsella

1

Today I put on a terrible strength invoking the Trinity, confessing the Three with faith in the One as I face my Maker.

2

Today I put on the power of Christ's birth and baptism of His hanging and burial, His resurrection, ascension and descent at the judgement.

3

Today I put on the power
of the order of Cherubim,
angels' obedience,
archangels' attendance,
in hope of ascending
to my reward;
patriarchs' prayers,
prophets' predictions,
apostles' precepts,
confessors' testimony,
holy virgins' testimony,
holy virgins' innocence
and the deeds of true men.

4

Today I put on the power of Heaven,
the light of the Sun,
the radiance of the Moon,
the splendour of fire,
the fierceness of lightning,
the swiftness of wind,
the depth of the sea,
the firmness of earth
and the hardness of rock.

5

Today I put on
God's strength to steer me,
God's power to uphold me,
God's wisdom to guide me,
God's eye for my vision,
God's ear for my hearing,
God's word for my speech,
God's hand to protect me,
God's pathway before me,
God's shield for my shelter,
God's angels to guard me,
from ambush of devils,
from vice's allurements,
from traps of the flesh,
from all who wish ill,
whether distant or close,
alone or in hosts.

I summon these powers today, [6]
to take my part against every implacable power
that attacks my body and soul,
the chants of false prophets,
dark laws of the pagans,
false heretics' laws,
entrapments of idols,
enchantments of women
or smiths or druids,
and all knowledge that poisons
man's body or soul.

Christ guard me today [7]
from poison, from burning,
from drowning, from hurt,
that I have my reward.

Christ beside me, [8]
Christ before me,
Christ behind me,
Christ within me,
Christ beneath me,
Christ above me,

Christ on my right hand, [9]
Christ on my left,

10

Christ where I lie,
Christ where I sit,
Christ where I rise,

11

Christ in the hearts of all who think of me,
Christ in the mouths of all who speak to me,
Christ in every eye that sees me,
Christ in every ear that hears me.

12

Today I put on
a terrible strength,
invoking the Trinity,
confessing the Three,
with faith in the One
as I face my Maker.

13

Domini est salus.
Domini est salus.
Domini est salus.
Salus tua, Domine,
sit semper vobiscum.

Saint Patrick's Breastplate

Today I put on
a terrible strength
invoking the Trinity,
confessing the Three
with faith in the One
as I face my Maker.

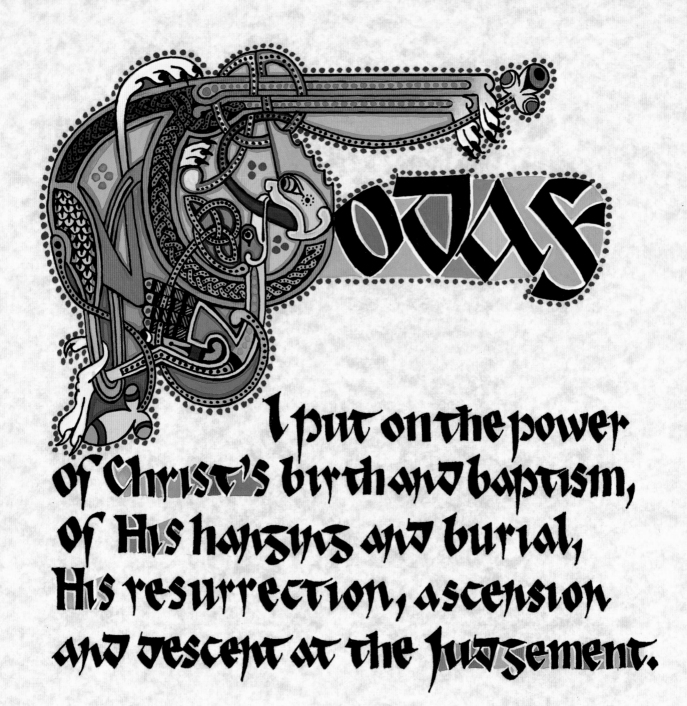

TODAY I put on the power of Christ's birth and baptism, of His hanging and burial, His resurrection, ascension and descent at the judgement.

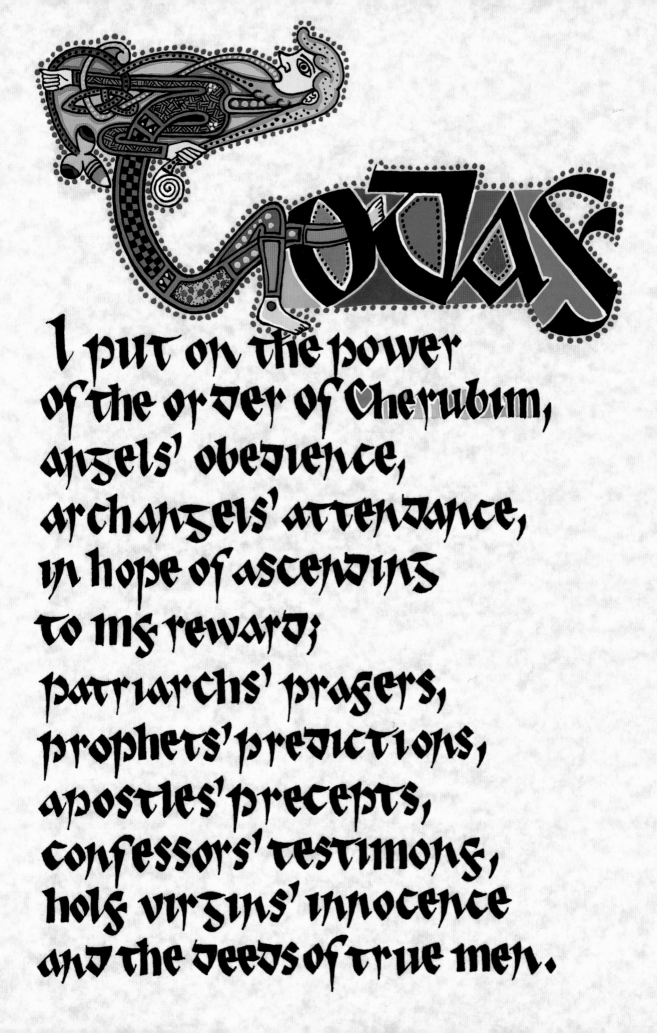

Todas

I put on the power
of the order of Cherubim,
angels' obedience,
archangels' attendance,
in hope of ascending
to my reward;
patriarchs' prayers,
prophets' predictions,
apostles' precepts,
confessors' testimony,
holy virgins' innocence
and the deeds of true men.

TODAY I put on
the power of Heaven,
the light of the Sun,
the radiance of the Moon,
the splendour of fire,
the fierceness of lightning,
the swiftness of wind,
the depth of the sea,
the firmness of earth
and the hardness of rock.

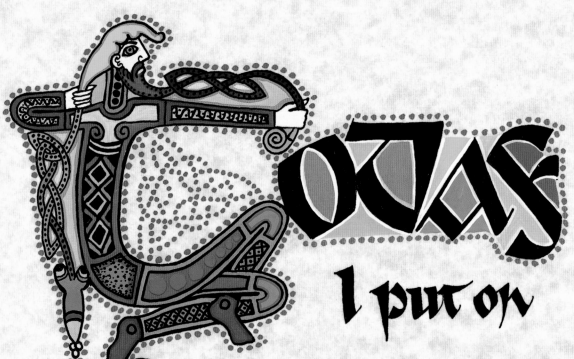

TODAY

I put on

God's strength to steer me,
God's power to uphold me,
God's wisdom to guide me,
God's eye for my vision,
God's ear for my hearing,
God's word for my speech,
God's hand to protect me,
God's pathway before me,

God's shield for my shelter,
God's angels to guard me,
from ambush of devils,
from vice's allurements,
from traps of the flesh,
from all who wish ill,
whether distant or close,
alone or in hosts.

I summon these powers today,
to take my part against
every implacable power
that attacks my body and
soul,
the chants of false prophets,
dark laws of the pagans,
false heretics' laws,
entrapments of idols,
enchantments of women
or smiths or druids,
and all knowledge that poisons
man's body and soul.

hrist guard me today
from poison, from burning,
from drowning, from hurt,
that I have my reward.

Christ beside me,
Christ before me,
Christ behind me,
Christ within me,
Christ beneath me,
Christ above me,

Christ on my right hand,
Christ on my left,

Christ where I lie,
Christ where I sit,
Christ where I rise,

Christ in the hearts of
all who think of me,
Christ in the mouths of all who
speak to me,
Christ in every eye that sees me,
Christ in every ear that hears me.

Today I put on
a terrible strength,
invoking the Trinity,
confessing the Three,
with faith in the One
as I face my Maker.

Domini est salus.
Domini est salus.
Domini est salus.
Salus tua, Domine,
sit semper vobiscum.

51

Crom Dubh

The Hill of the Eagles, Cruachan Aigli, is now more commonly called Croagh Patrick. It is an impressive, conical mountain on the west coast of Ireland, overlooking Westport in County Mayo. There are three main pilgrimages to the summit each year, and the one which takes place on the last Sunday of July is known as Domhnach Crom Dubh, or 'Black Crom's Sunday'.

The pagan chieftain, Crom Dubh, who lived in Connaught, was a good friend of St Patrick, and yet he refused to accept the Christian faith and to be baptized. Nevertheless, when he slaughtered one of his cattle for meat, he sent a quarter of the animal to the saint as a present. On his return, the servant who had delivered the generous gift was asked by Crom Dubh how Patrick had received it. 'All he said was "Deo Gratias" [meaning Thanks be to God]', said the man.

The chieftain was amazed at this, and so sent another quarter of the beast to see if this would evoke any more gratitude from Patrick. Again, the servant reported that the response had been exactly the same. A third quarter was sent in the hope that it would elicit a better reaction, and when it did not, the enraged Crom Dubh sent for St Patrick. Not only was he astonished, he was very angry at what he saw as the saint's lack of appreciation of his benevolence. He fully intended to kill Patrick for his ingratitude.

When confronted and reproached, St Patrick protested that he had indeed given the greatest thanks he could, and he called for a pair of scales to be brought. Three-quarters of an ox, similar to the meat received by Patrick was placed on one side, and in the other scale-pan the saint placed a piece of paper on which he had written the words 'Deo Gratias' three times. The paper weighed much more than the meat, and tipped the balance heavily. Crom Dubh was astounded and freely admitted his error of judgement. He agreed to be baptized, and asked for his household and followers to be included too.

St Patrick's Bell

During the season of Lent, before the great festival of Easter, it was St Patrick's custom to fast and pray for 40 days and 40 nights in an isolated place, following the examples of Moses and Jesus. One year he chose to do this on the magnificent peak of Croagh Patrick.

As his time of abstinence was coming to an end, the sky around him was darkened by a great flapping of menacing wings, and the air was filled with inky-black shapes which crowded in upon him so densely that he could see nothing beyond them. They were not birds but hellish fiends, which came screaming at him, stinking vilely, trying to injure and smother him. To defend himself Patrick recited psalms and sang hymns very loudly, hoping to keep them at bay; then he made the sign of the cross and rang his bell to banish them. It is said that the sound of his bell ringing could be heard all over Ireland. His actions proved unsuccessful and so, in desperation, he finally flung his bell at them, at which point they scattered and disappeared, plunging down the mountainside into a deep hollow called Log na Deamhan or 'Hollow of the Demons' – but the bell was cracked in its fall. The saint placed heavy rocks over the fiends' graves, driving them in with such force that water bubbled up and filled the dark hole. This sheet of water can still be seen at the north base of the cruach, the conical part of the mountain. Hosts of sweetly singing angels with pure white plumage appeared in place of the malevolent demons.

St Patrick's simple iron bell can be seen in the National Museum of Ireland in Dublin, along with the elaborate and beautiful bell-shrine which houses it. It is a very precious relic and was actually kept on Croagh Patrick for many years. According to a traditional story, the Clog Dubh Phadraig or 'Black Bell of St Patrick' was originally made of white metal, but because of the demons on the mountain constantly assailing it, it turned black. At one time it was used for swearing oaths in legal transactions, because it was thought that no one would dare to commit perjury on such a sacred object.

St Patrick and the Snakes

One of the most popular and well-known stories about St Patrick must be how he is credited with banishing all the snakes from Ireland.

Jocelyn, a Cistercian monk from Scotland writing in the twelfth century, says that since Ireland was first inhabited it had suffered from three great ills, a 'triple plague' as he calls it. These were: 'a great abundance of venomous reptiles; miriads of demons visibly appearing; and a multitude of magicians'.

St Patrick is said to have freed the land from its infestation of serpents when he was spending time on Croagh Patrick in prayer and penance. He took his pastoral staff, called Bachall Iosa, 'Staff of Jesus', in his hand, and with this symbol of his authority he ordered all the reptiles to be gone and hurled them down the mountain into Log na Deamhan, where he had previously flung the diabolical demons who had attacked him during a Lenten vigil.

In effect, this probably refers not to his mastery over the animal kingdom, but to his success in subduing and casting out other religions from Ireland. Although, interestingly, there are no snakes in Ireland today.

St Patrick and the Bull

After St Patrick's exertions and success in ridding Ireland of its population of serpents and chasing them into Log na Deamhan, he and his disciples were ravenously hungry and their appetites very sharp. They asked Crom Dubh for the gift of a bullock to feed themselves, but instead he offered them the prize of a ferocious bull. The animal was so savage that it would reputedly kill whoever approached it.

However, at Patrick's bidding it became docile and laid its head on the chopping block, offering itself for slaughter so that its meat might feed the saint and his followers. After giving thanks, they killed and skinned the beast, and, with great enjoyment, ate their fill until they were satisfied.

After some time, Crom Dubh requested the return of the bull, so Patrick instructed his men to gather all the bones together in one place and to put the hide of the beast on top, so that the bones were covered. St Patrick prayed over them and the bull came to life again, more bellicose than ever!

59

The *Confession* of Sτ Patrick

The most important sources we have for our knowledge and understanding of St Patrick are his own writings, and it is generally accepted by scholars and academics that both the *Letter to Coroticus* and the *Confession* are from the pen of the saint himself. The first is an open letter to Coroticus, a Christian chieftain who governed from Alt Clut, Strathclyde in Scotland. His warriors had crossed to Dalriada in Ireland and killed a group of newly baptized Christian converts, still dressed in their white baptismal robes, and Patrick, outraged at this event, wrote a strong epistle of accusation and reprimand to the king whom he held responsible.

The second text, called the *Confession*, is longer and, although it is not strictly speaking an autobiography, tells us far more about Patrick the man. He wrote it in his old age when he felt death approaching, and the final words of this text are, 'This is my Confession before I die', hence its name. It is not a confession of sins, or even theological beliefs, but rather the story of how St Patrick perceived God at work in his own life. There are autobiographical passages, but Patrick is far more concerned in showing the miraculous way in which God has dealt with him, and 'protected and comforted' him throughout his earthly existence. Although Patrick fully admits his lack of culture and learning, the *Confession* is written with great feeling and has a natural warmth and depth of expression in which the spirit of the man shines through. It is an invaluable document in our study of the saint.

The oldest copy of the *Confession* is contained in the *Book of Armagh* in the library of Trinity College, Dublin.

The Confession of Saint Patrick

The *Confession* of St Patrick

Translated from the Latin by Ludwig Bieler

1

I am Patrick, a sinner, most unlearned, the least of all the faithful, and utterly despised by many. My father was Calpornius, a deacon, son of Potitus, a priest, of the village Bannavem Taburniæ; he had a country seat nearby, and there I was taken captive.

2

I was then about sixteen years of age. I did not know the true God. I was taken into captivity to Ireland with many thousands of people – and deservedly so, because we turned away from God, and did not keep His commandments, and did not obey our priests, who used to remind us of our salvation. And the Lord brought over us the wrath of his anger and scattered us among many nations, even unto the utmost part of the earth, where now my littleness is placed among strangers.

3

And there the Lord opened the sense of my unbelief that I might at last remember my sins and be converted with all my heart to the Lord my God, who had regard for my abjection, and mercy on my youth and ignorance, and watched over me before I knew Him, and before I was able to distinguish between good and evil, and guarded me, and comforted me as would a father his son.

THE CONFESSION OF SAINT PATRICK

am Patrick, a sinner, most unlearned, least of all the faithfull, and utterly despised by many. My father was Calpornius, a deacon, son of Potitus, a priest, of the village Bannavem Taburniæ; he had a country seat nearby, and there I was taken captive.

I was then about sixteen years of age. I did not know the true God. I was taken into captivity to Ireland with many thousands of people ~ and deservedly so, because we turned away from God, and did not keep His commandments, and did not obey our priests, who used to remind us of our salvation. And the Lord brought over us the wrath of his anger and scattered us among many nations, even unto the utmost part of the earth, where now my littleness is placed among strangers.

ND there the Lord opened the sense of my unbelief that I might at last remember my sins and be converted with all my heart to the Lord my God, who had regard for my abjection, and mercy on my youth and ignorance, and watched over me before I knew Him, and before I was able to distinguish between good and evil, and guarded me, and comforted me as would a father his son.

4

Hence I cannot be silent – nor, indeed, is it expedient – about the great benefits and the great grace which the Lord has deigned to bestow upon me in the land of my captivity; for this we can give to God in return after having been chastened by Him, to exalt and praise His wonders before every nation that is anywhere under the heaven.

5

Because there is no other God, nor ever was, nor will be, than God the Father unbegotten, without beginning, from whom is all beginning, Lord of the universe, as we have been taught; and His son Jesus Christ, whom we declare to have always been with the Father, spiritually and ineffably begotten by the Father before the beginning of the world, before all beginning; and by Him are made all things visible and invisible. He was made man, and, having defeated death, was received into heaven by the Father; and He hath given Him all power over all names in heaven, on earth, and under the earth, and every tongue shall confess to Him that Jesus Christ is Lord and God, in whom we believe, and whose advent we expect soon to be, judge of the living and of the dead, who will render to every man according to his deeds; and He has poured forth upon us abundantly the Holy Spirit, the gift and pledge of immortality, who makes those who believe and obey sons of God and joint heirs with Christ; and Him do we confess and adore, one God in the Trinity of the Holy Name.

Hence I cannot be silent~nor, indeed, is it expedient~about the great benefits and the great grace which the Lord has deigned to bestow upon me in the land of my captivity; for this we can give to God in return after having been chastened by Him, to exalt and praise His wonders before every nation that is anywhere under the heaven.

ecause there is no other God,

nor ever was, nor will be, than God the Father unbegotten, without beginning, from whom is all beginning, Lord of the universe, as we have been taught; and His Son Jesus Christ, whom we declare to have always been with the Father, spiritually and ineffably begotten by the Father before the beginning of the world, before all beginning; and by Him are made all things visible and invisible. He was made man, and, having defeated death, was received into heaven by the Father; and He hath given Him all power over all names in heaven, on earth, and under the earth, and every tongue shall confess to Him that Jesus Christ is Lord and God, in whom we believe, and whose advent we expect soon to be, judge of the living and of the dead, who will render to every man according to his deeds; and He has poured forth upon us abundantly the Holy Spirit, the gift and pledge of immortality, who makes those who believe and obey sons of God and joint heirs with Christ; and Him do we confess and adore,

one God
in the Trinity of
the Holy Name:

6

For He Himself has said through the Prophet: Call upon me in the day of thy trouble, and I will deliver thee, and thou shalt glorify me. And again He says: It is honourable to reveal and confess the works of God.

7

Although I am imperfect in many things, I nevertheless wish that my brethren and kinsmen should know what sort of person I am, so that they may understand my heart's desire.

8

I know well the testimony of my Lord, who in the Psalm declares: Thou wilt destroy them that speak a lie. And again He says: The mouth that belieth killeth the soul. And the same Lord says in the Gospel: Every idle word that men shall speak, they shall render an account for it on the day of judgement.

9

And so I should dread exceedingly, with fear and trembling, this sentence on that day when no one will be able to escape or hide, but we all, without exception, shall have to give an account even of our smallest sins before the judgement of the Lord Christ.

10

For this reason I had in mind to write, but hesitated until now; I was afraid of exposing myself to the talk of men, because I have not studied like the others, who thoroughly imbibed law and Sacred Scripture, and never had to change from the language of their childhood days, but were able to make it still more perfect. In our case, what I had to say had to be translated into a tongue foreign to me, as can be easily proved from the savour of my writing, which betrays how little instruction and training I have had in the art of words; for, so says Scripture, by the tongue will be discovered the wise man, and understanding, and knowledge, and the teaching of truth.

72

For He Himself has said through the Prophet: Call upon me in the day of thy trouble, and I will deliver thee, and thou shalt glorify me. And again He says: It is honourable to reveal and confess the works of God.

Although I am imperfect in many things, I nevertheless wish that my brethren and kinsmen should know what sort of person I am, so that they may understand my heart's desire.

Know well the testimony of my Lord, who in the Psalm declares: Thou wilt destroy them that speak a lie. And again He says: The mouth that belieth killeth the soul. And the same Lord says in the Gospel: Every idle word that men shall speak, they shall render an account for it on the day of judgement.

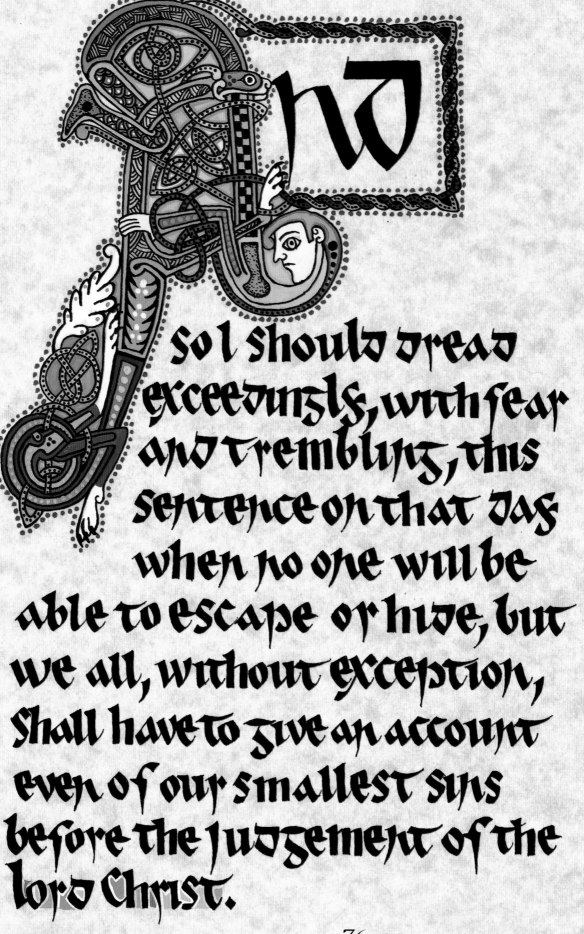

nd so I should dread exceedingly, with fear and trembling, this sentence on that day when no one will be able to escape or hide, but we all, without exception, shall have to give an account even of our smallest sins before the judgement of the lord Christ.

11

But of what help is an excuse, however true, especially if combined with presumption, since now, in my old age, I strive for something that I did not acquire in youth? It was my sins that prevented me from fixing in my mind what before I had barely read through. But who believes me, though I should repeat what I started out with?

12

As a youth, nay, almost as a boy not able to speak, I was taken captive, before I knew what to pursue and what to avoid. Hence today I blush and fear exceedingly to reveal my lack of education; for I am unable to tell my story to those versed in the art of concise writing – in such a way, I mean, as my spirit and mind long to do, and so that the sense of my words expresses what I feel.

13

But if indeed it had been given to me as it was given to others, then I would not be silent because of my desire of thanksgiving; and if perhaps some people think me arrogant for doing so in spite of my lack of knowledge and my slow tongue, it is, after all, written: The stammering tongues shall quickly learn to speak peace.

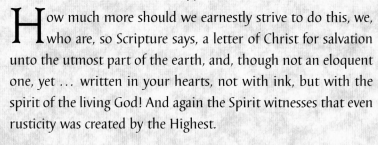

14

How much more should we earnestly strive to do this, we, who are, so Scripture says, a letter of Christ for salvation unto the utmost part of the earth, and, though not an eloquent one, yet … written in your hearts, not with ink, but with the spirit of the living God! And again the Spirit witnesses that even rusticity was created by the Highest.

15

Whence I, once rustic, exiled, unlearned, who does not know how to provide for the future, this at least I know most certainly that before I was humiliated I was like a stone lying in the deep mire; and He that is mighty came and in His mercy lifted me up, and raised me aloft, and placed me on the top of the wall. And therefore I ought to cry out aloud and so also render something to the Lord for His great benefits here and in eternity – benefits which the mind of men is unable to appraise.

16

Wherefore, then, be astonished, ye great and little that fear God, and you men of letters on your estates, listen and pore over this. Who was it that roused up me, the fool that I am, from the midst of those who in the eyes of men are wise, and expert in law, and powerful in word and in everything? And He inspired me – me, the outcast of this world – before others, to be the man (if only I could!) who, with fear and reverence and without blame, should faithfully serve the people to whom the love of Christ conveyed and gave me for the duration of my life, if I should be worthy; yes indeed, to serve them humbly and sincerely.

17

In the light, therefore, of our faith in the Trinity I must make this choice, regardless of danger I must make known the gift of God and everlasting consolation, without fear and frankly I must spread everywhere the name of God so that after my decease I may leave a bequest to my brethren and sons whom I have baptised in the Lord – so many thousands of people.

18

And I was not worthy, nor was I such that the Lord should grant this to His servant; that after my misfortunes and so great difficulties, after my captivity, after the lapse of so many years, He should give me so great a grace on behalf of that nation – a thing which once, in my youth, I never expected nor thought of.

19

But after I came to Ireland – every day I had to tend sheep, and many times a day I prayed – the love of God and His fear came to me more and more, and my faith was strengthened. And my spirit was moved so that in a single day I would say as many as a hundred prayers, and almost as many in the night, and this even when I was staying in the woods and on the mountains; and I used to get up for prayer before daylight, through snow, through frost, through rain, and I felt no harm, and there was no sloth in me – as I now see, because the spirit within me was then fervent.

In the light, therefore, of our faith in the Trinity I must make this choice, regardless of danger I must make known the gift of God and everlasting consolation, without fear and frankly I must spread everywhere the name of god so that after my decease I may leave a bequest to my brethren and sons whome I have baptised in the lord~ so many thousands of people.

UT after I came to Ireland – every day I had to tend sheep, and many times a day I prayed – the love of God and His fear came to me more and more, and my faith was strengthened.

and my spirit was moved so
that in a single day I would say
as many as a hundred prayers,
and almost as many in the night,
and this even when I was
staying in the woods and on the
mountains; and I used to get
up for prayer before daylight,
through snow, through frost,
through rain, and I felt no
harm, and there was no sloth in
me—as I now see, because the
spirit within me was then
fervent.

20

And there one night I heard in my sleep a voice saying to me: 'It is well that you fast, soon you will go to your own country.' And again, after a short while, I heard a voice saying to me: 'See, your ship is ready.' And it was not near, but at a distance of perhaps two hundred miles, and I had never been there, nor did I know a living soul there; and then I took to flight, and I left the man with whom I had stayed for six years. And I went in the strength of God who directed my way to my good, and I feared nothing until I came to that ship.

21

And the day that I arrived the ship was set afloat, and I said that I was able to pay for my passage with them. But the captain was not pleased, and with indignation he answered harshly: 'It is of no use for you to ask us to go along with us.' And when I heard this, I left them in order to return to the hut where I was staying. And as I went, I began to pray; and before I had ended my prayer, I heard one of them shouting behind me, 'Come, hurry, we shall take you on in good faith; make friends with us in whatever way you like.' And so on that day I refused to suck their breasts for fear of God, but rather hoped they would come to the faith of Jesus Christ, because they were pagans. And thus I had my way with them, and we set sail at once.

22

And after three days we reached land, and for twenty-eight days we travelled through deserted country. And they lacked food, and hunger overcame them; and the next day the captain said to me: 'Tell me, Christian: you say that your God is great and all-powerful; why, then, do you not pray for us? As you can see, we are suffering from hunger; it is unlikely indeed that we shall ever see a human being again.'

23

I said to them full of confidence: 'Be truly converted with all your heart to the Lord my God, because nothing is impossible for Him, that this day He may send you food on your way until you be satisfied; for He has abundance everywhere.' And, with the help of God, so it came to pass: suddenly a herd of pigs appeared on the road before our eyes, and they killed many of them; and there they stopped for two nights and fully recovered their strength, and their hounds received their fill for many of them had grown weak and were half-dead along the way. And from that day they had plenty of food. They also found wild honey, and offered some of it to me, and one of them said: 'This we offer in sacrifice.' Thanks be to God, I tasted none of it.

24

That same night, when I was asleep, Satan assailed me violently, a thing I shall remember as long as I shall be in this body. And he fell upon me like a huge rock, and I could not stir a limb. But whence came it into my mind, ignorant as I am, to call upon Helias? And meanwhile I saw the sun rise in the sky, and while I was shouting 'Helias! Helias' with all my might, suddenly the splendour of that sun fell on me and immediately freed me of all misery. And I believe that I was sustained by Christ my Lord, and that His Spirit was even then crying out on my behalf, and I hope it will be so on the day of my tribulation, as is written in the Gospel: On that day, the Lord declares, it is not you that speak, but the Spirit of your Father that speaketh in you.

25

And once again, after many years, I fell into captivity. On that first night I stayed with them, I heard a divine message saying to me: 'Two months will you be with them.' And so it came to pass: on the sixtieth night thereafter the Lord delivered me out of their hands.

That

same night, when
I was asleep, Satan assailed me
violently, a thing I shall
remember as long as I shall be in
this body. And he fell upon me
like a huge rock, and I could
not stir a limb.

But whence came it into my mind, ignorant as I am, to call upon Helias? and meanwhile I saw the sun rise in the sky, and while I was shouting 'Helias! Helias' with all my might, suddenly the splendour of that sun fell on me and immediately freed me of all misery. And I believe that I was sustained by Christ my lord, and that His Spirit was even then crying out on my behalf, and I hope it will be so on the day of my tribulation, as is written in the Gospel:

On that day, the lord
declares, it is not you that
speak, but the Spirit of your
Father that speaketh in you.

26

Also on our way God gave us food and fire and dry weather every day, until, on the tenth day, we met people. As I said above, we travelled twenty-eight days through deserted country, and the night that we met people we had no food left.

27

And again after a few years I was in Britain with my people who received me as their son, and sincerely besought me that now at last, having suffered so many hardships, I should not leave them and go elsewhere.

28

And there I saw in the night the vision of a man, whose name was Victoricus, coming as it were from Ireland, with countless letters. And he gave me one of them, and I read the opening words of the letter, which were, 'The voice of the Irish'; and as I read the beginning of the letter I thought that at the same moment I heard their voice – they were those beside the Wood of Voclut, which is near the Western Sea – and thus did they cry out as with one mouth: 'We ask thee, boy, come and walk among us once more.'

29

And I was quite broken in heart, and could read no further, and so I woke up. Thanks be to God, after many years the Lord gave to them according to their cry.

30

And another night – whether within me, or beside me, I know not, God knoweth – they called me most unmistakably with words which I heard but could not understand, except that at the end of the prayer He spoke thus: 'He that has laid down His life for thee, it is He that speaketh in thee'; and so I awoke full of joy.

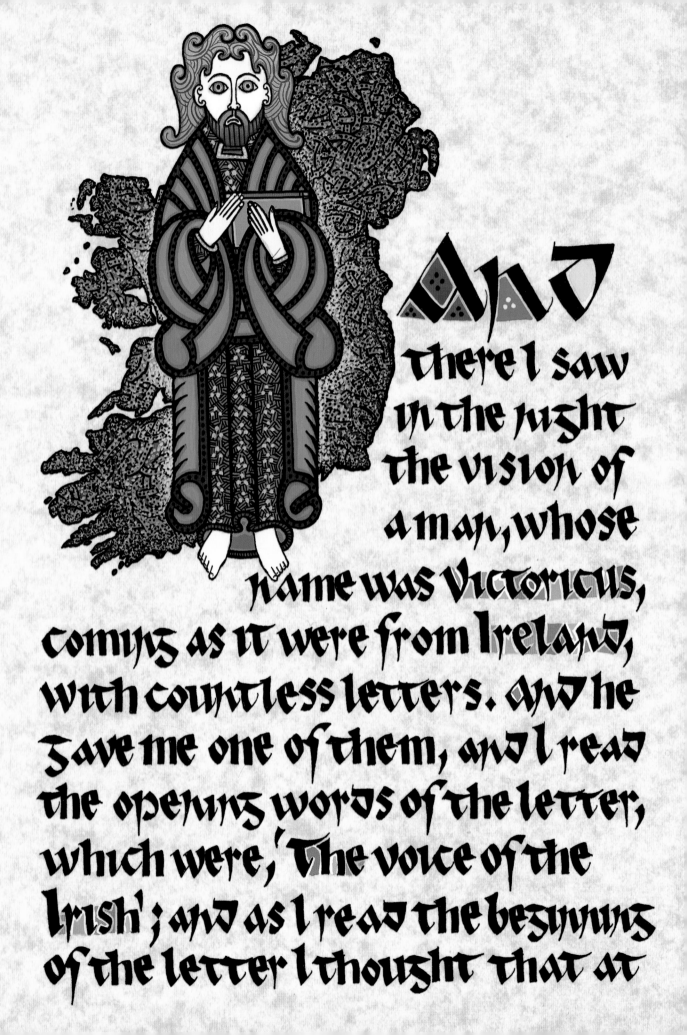

And there I saw in the night the vision of a man, whose name was Victoricus, coming as it were from Ireland, with countless letters. And he gave me one of them, and I read the opening words of the letter, which were, 'The voice of the Irish'; and as I read the beginning of the letter I thought that at the same moment I heard their voice - they were those beside the Wood of Voclut, which is near the western Sea - and thus did they cry out as with one mouth:

'we ask thee, boy, come and walk among us once more'.

ND another night—
whether within me,
or beside me, I know
not, God knoweth—they
called me most unmistakably
with words which I heard but
could not understand, except
that at the end of the prayer
He spoke thus:

He that has laid down His life for thee, it is He that speaketh in thee'; and so I awoke full of joy.

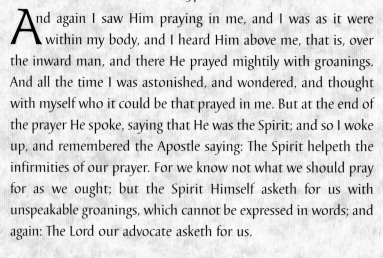

31

And again I saw Him praying in me, and I was as it were within my body, and I heard Him above me, that is, over the inward man, and there He prayed mightily with groanings. And all the time I was astonished, and wondered, and thought with myself who it could be that prayed in me. But at the end of the prayer He spoke, saying that He was the Spirit; and so I woke up, and remembered the Apostle saying: The Spirit helpeth the infirmities of our prayer. For we know not what we should pray for as we ought; but the Spirit Himself asketh for us with unspeakable groanings, which cannot be expressed in words; and again: The Lord our advocate asketh for us.

32

And when I was attacked by a number of my seniors who came forth and brought up my sins against my laborious episcopate, on that day indeed was I struck so that I might have fallen now and for eternity; but the Lord graciously spared the stranger and sojourner for His name and came mightily to my help in this affliction. Verily, not slight was the shame and blame that fell upon me! I ask God that it may not be reckoned to them as sin.

33

As cause for proceeding against me they found - after thirty years! - a confession I had made before I was a deacon. In the anxiety of my troubled mind I confided to my dearest friend what I had done in my boyhood one day, nay, in one hour, because I was not yet strong. I know not, God knoweth - whether I was then fifteen years old: and I did not believe in the living God, nor did I so from my childhood, but lived in death and unbelief until I was severely chastised and really humiliated, by hunger and nakedness, and that daily.

34

On the other hand, I did not go to Ireland of my own accord, not until I had nearly perished; but this was rather for my good, for thus was I purged by the Lord; and He made me fit so that I might be now what was once far from me that I should care and labour for the salvation of others, whereas then I did not even care about myself.

35

On that day, then, when I was rejected by those referred to and mentioned above, in that night I saw a vision of the night. There was a writing without honour against my face, and at the same time I heard God's voice saying to me: 'We have seen with displeasure the face of Deisignatus' (thus revealing his name). He did not say, 'Thou hast seen,' but 'We have seen,' as if He included Himself, as He sayeth: He who toucheth you toucheth as it were the apple of my eye.

36

Therefore I give Him thanks who hath strengthened me in everything, as He did not frustrate the journey upon which I had decided, and the work which I had learned from Christ my Lord; but I rather felt after this no little strength, and my trust was proved right before God and men.

Therefore
I give Him thanks who hath
strengthened me in everything,
as He did not frustrate the
journey upon which I had
decided, and the work which I
had learned from Christ my
lord; but I rather felt after
this no little strength, and my
trust was proved right before
God and men.

37

And so I say boldly, my conscience does not blame me now or in the future: God is my witness that I have not lied in the account which I have given you.

38

But the more am I sorry for my dearest friend that we had to hear what he said. To him I had confided my very soul! And I was told by some of the brethren before that defence – at which I was not present, nor was I in Britain, nor was it suggested by me – that he would stand up for me in my absence. He had even said to me in person: 'Look, you should be raised to the rank of bishop!' – of which I was not worthy. But whence did it come to him afterwards that he let me down before all, good and evil, and publicly, in a matter in which he had favoured me before spontaneously and gladly – and not he alone, but the Lord, who is greater than all?

39

Enough of this. I must not, however, hide God's gift which He bestowed upon me in the land of my captivity; because then I earnestly sought Him, and there I found Him, and He saved me from all evil because – so I believe – of His Spirit that dwelleth in me. Again, boldly said. But God knows it, had this been said to me by a man, I had perhaps remained silent for the love of Christ.

And so I say boldly, my conscience does not blame me now or the future: God is my witness that I have not lied in the account which I have given you.

40

Hence, then, I give unwearied thanks to God, who kept me faithful in the day of my temptation, so that today I can confidently offer Him my soul as a living sacrifice – to Christ my Lord, who saved me out of all my troubles. Thus I can say: 'Who am I, O Lord, and to what hast Thou called me, Thou who didst assist me with such divine power that today I constantly exalt and magnify Thy name among the heathens wherever I may be, and not only in good days but also in tribulations?' So indeed I must accept with equanimity whatever befalls me, be it good or evil, and always give thanks to God, who taught me to trust in Him always without hesitation, and who must have heard my prayer so that I, however ignorant I was, in the last days dared to undertake such a holy and wonderful work – thus imitating somehow those who, as the Lord once foretold, would preach His Gospel for a testimony to all nations before the end of the world. So we have seen it, and so it has been fulfilled: indeed, we are witnesses that the Gospel has been preached unto those parts beyond which there lives nobody.

41

Now, it would be tedious to give a detailed account of all my labours or even a part of them. Let me tell you briefly how the merciful God often freed me from slavery and from twelve dangers in which my life was at stake – not to mention numerous plots, which I cannot express in words; for I do not want to bore my readers. But God is my witness, who knows all things even before they come to pass, as He used to forewarn even me, poor wretch that I am, of many things by a divine message.

42

How came I by this wisdom, which was not in me, who neither knew the number of my days nor knew what God was? Whence was given to me afterwards the gift so great, so salutary – to know God and to love Him, although at the price of leaving my country and my parents?

OW came I by this wisdom, which was not in me, who neither knew the number of my days nor knew what God was? whence was given to me afterwards the gift so great, so salutary—to know God and to love Him, although at the price of leaving my country and my parents?

43

And many gifts were offered to me in sorrow and tears, and I offended the donors, much against the wishes of some of my seniors; but, guided by God, in no way did I agree with them or acquiesce. It was not grace of my own, but God, who is strong in me and resists them all – as He had done when I came to the people of Ireland to preach the Gospel, and to suffer insult from the unbelievers, hearing the reproach of my going abroad, and many persecutions even unto bonds, and to give my free birth for the benefit of others; and, should I be worthy, I am prepared to give even my life without hesitation and most gladly for His name, and it is there that I wish to spend it until I die, if the Lord would grant it to me.

44

For I am very much God's debtor, who gave me such grace that many people were reborn in God through me and afterwards confirmed, and that clerics were ordained for them everywhere, for a people just coming to the faith, whom the Lord took from the utmost parts of the earth, as He once had promised through His prophets: To Thee the gentiles shall come from the ends of the earth and shall say: 'How false are the idols that our fathers got for themselves, and there is no profit in them'; and again: 'I have set Thee as a light among the gentiles, that Thou mayest be for salvation unto the utmost part of the earth.'

45

And there I wish to wait for His promise who surely never deceives, as He promises in the Gospel: They shall come from the east and the west, and shall sit down with Abraham and Isaac and Jacob – as we believe the faithful will come from all the world.

For I am very much God's debtor, who gave me such grace that many people were reborn in God through me and afterwards confirmed, and that clerics were ordained for them everywhere, for a people just coming to the faith, whome the Lord took from the utmost parts of the earth, as He once had promised through His prophets: To Thee the gentiles shall come from the ends of the earth and shall say: 'How false are the idols that our fathers got for themselves, and there is no profit in them'; and again: 'I have set Thee as a light among the gentiles, that Thou mayest be for salvation unto the utmost part of the earth'.

AND there I wish to wait for His promise who surely never deceives, as He promises in the Gospel: They shall come from the east and the west, and shall sit down with Abraham, Issac and Jacob~as we believe the faithfull will come from all the world.

46

For that reason, therefore, we ought to fish well and diligently, as the Lord exhorts in advance and teaches, saying: Come ye after me, and I will make you to be fishers of men. And again He says through the prophets: Behold, I send many fishers and hunters, saith God, and so on. Hence it was most necessary to spread our nets so that a great multitude and throng might be caught for God, and that there be clerics everywhere to baptise and exhort a people in need and want, as the Lord in the Gospel states, exhorts and teaches, saying: Going therefore now, teach ye all nations, baptising them in the name of the Father, and the Son, and the Holy Spirit, teaching them to observe all things whatsoever I have commanded you: and behold I am with you all days even to the consummation of the world. And again He says: Go ye therefore into the whole world, and preach the Gospel to every creature. He that believeth and is baptised shall be saved; but he that believeth not shall be condemned. And again: This Gospel of the kingdom shall be preached in the whole world for a testimony to all nations, and then shall come the end. And so too the Lord announces through the prophet, and says: And it shall come to pass, in the last days, saith the Lord, I will pour out of my Spirit upon all flesh; and your sons and your daughters shall prophesy, and your young men shall see visions, and your old men shall dream dreams. And upon my servants indeed, and upon my handmaids will I pour out in those days of my Spirit, and they shall prophesy. And in Osee, He saith: 'I will call that which was not my people, my people; … and her that had not obtained mercy, one that hath obtained mercy. And it shall be in the place where it was said: '"You are not my people," there they shall be called the sons of the living God.'

47

Hence, how did it come to pass in Ireland that those who never had a knowledge of God, but until now always worshipped idols and things impure, have now been made a people of the Lord, and are called sons of God, that the sons and daughters of the kings of the Irish are seen to be monks and virgins of Christ?

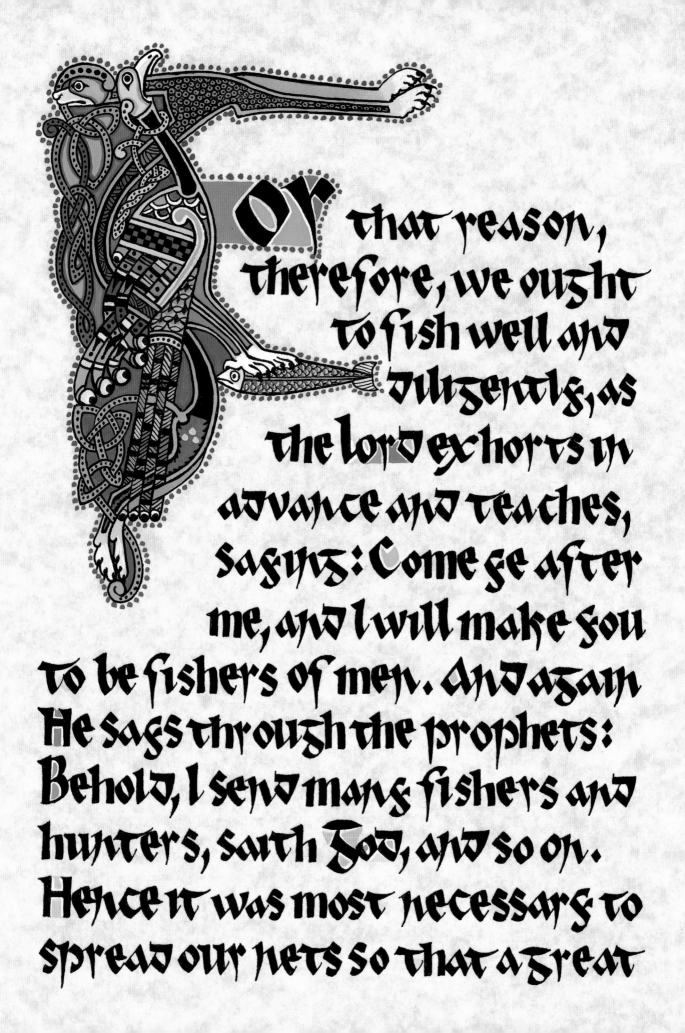

For that reason, therefore, we ought to fish well and diligently, as the Lord exhorts in advance and teaches, saying: Come ye after me, and I will make you to be fishers of men. And again He says through the prophets: Behold, I send many fishers and hunters, saith God, and so on. Hence it was most necessary to spread our nets so that a great

Hence, how did it come to pass in Ireland that those who never had a knowledge of God, but until now always worshipped idols and things impure, have now been made a people of the Lord, and are called sons of God, that the sons and daughters of the kings of the Irish are seen to monks and virgins of Christ?

48

Among others, a blessed Irishwoman of noble birth, beautiful, full-grown, whom I had baptised, came to us after some days for a particular reason: she told us that she had received a message from a messenger of God, and he admonished her to be a virgin of Christ and draw near to God. Thanks be to God, on the sixth day after this she most laudably and eagerly chose what all virgins of Christ do. Not that their fathers agree with them: no – they often ever suffer persecution and undeserved reproaches from their parents; and yet their number is ever increasing. How many have been reborn there so as to be of our kind, I do not know – not to mention widows and those who practice continence.

49

But greatest is the suffering of those women who live in slavery. All the time they have to endure terror and threats. But the Lord gave His grace to many of His maidens; for, though they are forbidden to do so, they follow Him bravely.

50

Wherefore, then, even if I wished to leave them and go to Britain – and how I would have loved to go to my country and my parents, and also to Gaul in order to visit the brethren and to see the face of the saints of my Lord! God knows it! That I much desired it; but I am bound by the Spirit, who gives evidence against me if I do this, telling me that I shall be guilty; and I am afraid of losing the labour which I have begun – nay, not I, but Christ the Lord who bade me come here and stay with them for the rest of my life, if the Lord will, and will guard me from every evil way that I may not sin before Him.

ut greatest is the suffering of those women who live in slavery. All the time they have to endure terror and threats. But the lord gave His grace to many of His maidens; for though they are forbidden to do so, they follow Him bravely.

51

This, I presume, I ought to do, but I do not trust myself as long as I am in this body of death, for strong is he who daily strives to turn me away from the faith and the purity of true religion to which I have devoted myself to the end of my life to Christ my Lord. But the hostile flesh is ever dragging us unto death, that is, towards the forbidden satisfaction of one's desires; and I know that in part I did not lead a perfect life as did the other faithful; but I acknowledge it to my Lord, and do not blush before Him, because I lie not: from the time I came to know Him in my youth, the love of God and the fear of Him have grown in me, and up to now, thanks to the grace of God, I have kept the faith.

52

And let those who will, laugh and scorn - I shall not be silent; nor shall I hide the signs and wonders which the Lord has shown me many years before they came to pass, as He knows everything even before the times of the world.

53

Hence I ought unceasingly to give thanks to God who often pardoned my folly and my carelessness, and on more than one occasion spared His great wrath on me, who was chosen to be His helper and who was slow to do as was shown me and as the Spirit suggested. And the Lord had mercy on me thousands and thousands of times because He saw that I was ready, but that I did not know what to do in the circumstances. For many tried to prevent this my mission; they would even talk to each other behind my back and say: 'Why does this fellow throw himself into danger among enemies who have no knowledge of God?' It was not malice, but it did not appeal to them because - and to this I own myself - of my rusticity. And I did not realise at once the grace that was then in me; now I understand that I should have done so before.

54

Now I have given a simple account to my brethren and fellow servants who have believed me because of what I said and still say in order to strengthen and confirm your faith. Would that you, too, would strive for greater things and do better! This will be my glory, for a wise son is the glory of his father.

55

You know, and so does God, how I have lived among you from my youth in the true faith and in sincerity of heart. Likewise, as regards the heathen among whom I live, I have been faithful to them, and so I shall be. God knows it, I have overreached none of them, nor would I think of doing so, for the sake of God and His Church, for fear of raising persecution against them and all of us, and for fear that through me the name of the Lord be blasphemed; for it is written: Woe to the man through whom the name of the Lord is blasphemed.

56

For although I be rude in all things, nevertheless I have tried somehow to keep myself safe, and that, too, for my Christian brethren, and the virgins of Christ, and the pious women who of their own accord made me gifts and laid on the altar some of their ornaments and I gave them back to them, and they were offended that I did so. But I did it for the hope of lasting success – in order to preserve myself cautiously in everything so that they might not seize upon me or the ministry of my service, under the pretext of dishonesty, and that I would not even in the smallest matter give the infidels an opportunity to defame or defile.

57

When I baptised so many thousands of people, did I perhaps expect from any of them as much as half a scruple? Tell me, and I will restore it to you. Or when the Lord ordained clerics everywhere through my unworthy person and I conferred the ministry upon them free, if I asked any of them as much as the price of my shoes, speak against me and I will return it to you.

58

On the contrary, I spent money for you that they might receive me; and I went to you and everywhere for your sake in many dangers, even to the farthest districts, beyond which there lived nobody and where nobody had ever come to baptise, or to ordain clergy, or to confirm the people. With the grace of the Lord, I did everything lovingly and gladly for your salvation.

59

All the while I used to give presents to the kings, besides the fees I paid to their sons who travel with me. Even so they laid hands on me and my companions, and on that day they eagerly wished to kill me; but my time had not yet come and everything they found with us they took away, and me they put in irons; and on the fourteenth day the Lord delivered me from their power, and our belongings were returned to us because of God and our dear friends whom we had seen before.

60

You know how much I paid to those who administered justice in all those districts to which I came frequently. I think I distributed among them not less than the price of fifteen men, so that you might enjoy me, and I might always enjoy you in God. I am not sorry for it – indeed it is not enough for me; I still spend and shall spend more. God has power to grant me afterwards that I myself may be spent for your souls.

61

Indeed, I call God to witness upon my soul that I lie not; neither, I hope, am I writing to you in order to make this an occasion of flattery or covetousness, nor because I look for honour from any of you. Sufficient is the honour that is not yet seen but is anticipated in the heart. Faithful is He that promised; He never lieth.

62

But I see myself exalted even in the present world beyond measure by the Lord, and I was not worthy nor such that He should grant me this. I know perfectly well, though not by my own judgement, that poverty and misfortune becomes me better than riches and pleasures. For Christ the Lord, too, was poor for our sakes; and I, unhappy wretch that I am, have no wealth even if I wished for it. Daily I expect murder, fraud, or captivity, or whatever it may be; but I fear none of these things because of the promises of heaven. I have cast myself into the hands of God Almighty, who rules everywhere, as the prophet says: Cast thy thought upon God, and He shall sustain thee.

63

So, now I commend my soul to my faithful God, for whom I am an ambassador in all my wretchedness; but God accepteth no person, and chose me for this office – to be, although among His least, one of His ministers.

64

Hence let me render unto Him for all He has done to me. But what can I say or what can I promise to my Lord, as I can do nothing that He has not given me? May He search the hearts and deepest feelings; for greatly and exceedingly do I wish, and ready I was, that He should give me His chalice to drink, as He gave it also to the others who loved Him.

O, now I commend my soul to my faithful God, for whom I am an ambassador in all wretchedness; but God accepteth no person, and chose me for this office — to be, although among His least, one of His ministers.

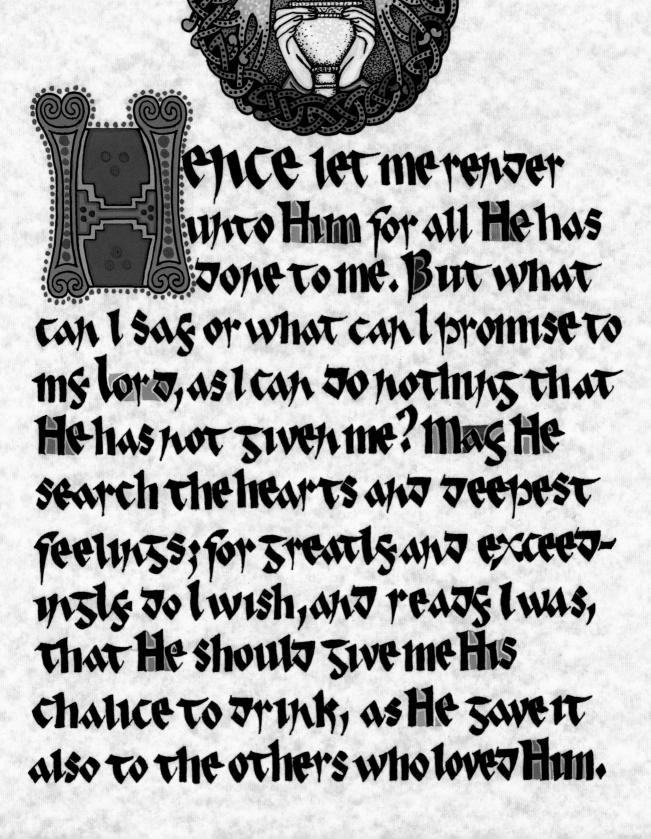

Hence let me render unto Him for all He has done to me. But what can I say or what can I promise to my lord, as I can do nothing that He has not given me? May He search the hearts and deepest feelings; for greatly and exceedingly do I wish, and ready I was, that He should give me His chalice to drink, as He gave it also to the others who loved Him.

Wherefore may God never permit it to happen to me that I should lose His people which He purchased in the utmost parts of the world. I pray to God to give me perseverance and to deign that I be a faithful witness to Him to the end of my life for my God.

65

Wherefore may God never permit it to happen to me that I should lose His people which He purchased in the utmost parts of the world. I pray to God to give me perseverance and to deign that I be a faithful witness to Him to the end of my life for my God.

66

And if ever I have done any good for my God whom I love, I beg Him to grant me that I may shed my blood with those exiles and captives for His name, even though I should be denied a grave, or my body be woefully torn to pieces limb by limb by hounds or wild beasts, or the fowls of the air devour it. I am firmly convinced that if this should happen to me, I would have gained my soul together with my body, because on that day without doubt we shall rise in the brightness of the sun, that is, in the glory of Christ Jesus our Redeemer, as sons of the living God and joint heirs with Christ, to be made conformable to His image; for of Him, and by Him, and in Him we shall reign.

67

For this sun which we see rises daily for us because He commands so, but it will never reign, nor will its splendour last; what is more, those wretches who adore it will be miserably punished. Not so we, who believe in, and worship, the true sun – Christ – who will never perish, nor will he who doeth His will; but he will abide for ever as Christ abideth for ever, who reigns with God the Father Almighty and the Holy Spirit before time, and now, and in all eternity. Amen.

And if ever I have done any good for my God whom I love, I beg Him to grant me that I may shed my blood with those exiles and captives for His name, even though I should be denied a grave, or my body be woefully torn to pieces limb by limb by hounds or wild beasts, or the fowls of the air devour it. I am firmly convinced that if this should happen to me, I would have gained my soul together with my body, because on that day without doubt we shall rise in the brightness of the sun, that is, in the glory of Christ Jesus our Redeemer, as sons of the living God and joint heirs with Christ, to be made comformable to His image; for of Him, and by Him, and in Him we shall reign.

For this sun which we see rises daily for us because He command so, but it will never reign, nor will its splendour last; what is more, those wretches who adore it will be miserably punished. Not so we, who believe in, and worship, the true sun – Christ – who will never perish, nor will he who doeth His will; but he will abide for ever as Christ abideth for ever, who reigns with God the Father Almighty and the Holy Spirit before time, and now, and in all eternity.

Amen.

ehold, again and again
would I set forth the
words of my confession.
I testify in truth and in joy of
heart before God and His holy
angels that I never had any
reason except the Gospel and
its promises why I should ever
return to the people from whom
once before I barely escaped.

68

Behold, again and again would I set forth the words of my confession. I testify in truth and in joy of heart before God and His holy angels that I never had any reason except the Gospel and its promises why I should ever return to the people from whom once before I barely escaped.

69

I pray those who believe and fear God, whosoever deigns to look at or receive this writing which Patrick, a sinner, unlearned, has composed in Ireland, that no one should ever say that it was my ignorance if I did or showed forth anything however small according to God's good pleasure; but let this be your conclusion and let it so be thought, that – as is the perfect truth – it was the gift of God. This is my confession before I die.

This is my confession
before I die.

Further Reading

Books by Courtney Davis

Celtic Art of Courtney Davis, Spirit of Celtia, 1985

The Celtic Art Source Book, Blandford, 1985

The Celtic Tarot, Aquarian, 1990

Celtic Design and Motifs, Dover, 1991

Celtic Borders and Decoration, Blandford, 1992

The Celtic Mandala Book, Blandford, 1993

The Art of Celtia, Blandford, 1994

The Book of Celtic Saints, Blandford, 1995

The Return of King Arthur, Blandford, 1995

The Celtic Image, Blandford, 1996

Celtic Ornament, Blandford, 1996

Celtic Initials and Alphabets, Blandford, 1997

Celtic Illumination – The Irish School, Thames and Hudson, 1998

Books by Other Authors

HENDERSON, George,
From Durrow to Kells, Thames and Hudson, 1987

HENRY, Francoise,
— *Irish Art*, Methuen, 1967
— *Irish Art in the Romanesque Period*, Methuen, 1970

LAING, Lloyd and Jennifer,
Art of the Celts, Thames and Hudson, 1992

MEEHAN, Bernard,
The Book of Kells, Thames and Hudson, 1994

NORDENFALK, Carl,
Celtic and Anglo-Saxon Painting, Chatto and Windus, 1977

QUILLER, Peter, and DAVIS, Courtney,
— *Merlin Awakes*, Firebird Books, 1990
— *Merlin the Immortal*, Spirit of Celtia, 1987

ROBERTS, Forrester, and DAVIS, Courtney,
Symbols of the Grail Quest, Spirit of Celtia, 1990

ROMILLY, Allen, J.,
Celtic Art in Pagan and Christian Times, Methuen, 1993

Further details on the work of Courtney Davis can be found on his Internet web page: www.celtic-art.com

Index